Contents

Boyling Point

political cartoons
by Frank Boyle

Argyll
publishing

First published 2006
Argyll Publishing
Glendaruel
Argyll PA22 3AE
Scotland
www.argyllpublishing.com

The author has asserted his moral rights.

**British Library Cataloguing-in-Publication Data.
A catalogue record for this book is available
from the British Library.**

ISBN 1 902831 47 0

Printing Bell & Bain Ltd, Glasgow

In memory of Frances Boyle (1923–2005)
and Canon Daniel J Boyle (1918–2006) R.I.P.

Foreword

This is my second collection of cartoons from the Edinburgh Evening News. The first, Hooray for Holyrood, was published in 2002 and in response to reader demand, it seemed like the right time to produce another one.

The cartoons in this new book cover most of the second term of the Scottish Parliament but overshadowing the whole period has been the war in Iraq and this is reflected in the number of drawings on the subject.

One of the good things about working for the Evening News is that I don't always have to cover national or international news. Local stories often produce some of the best results. It's surprising how many cartoons have been inspired by wheelie bins, road tolls and the fortunes of Hearts and Hibs.

I would like to thank the editor of the Evening News, John McLellan, and his predecessor Ian Stewart for all their support. I would also like to thank Derek Rodger of Argyll Publishing for all his efforts in producing the book.

Jack McConnell has urged Scots to lose their negativity and to talk ourselves up. In the spirit of this newly confident Scotland, can I paraphrase the First Minister and welcome you to the best small cartoon book in the world?

Frank Boyle
October 2006

2003

MTV Music Awards are held in Leith.

Due to lack of sperm donors in Scotland, sperm has to be imported from London at £75 a time.

Bacteria in water causes illness. Scottish Water directors get huge bonuses.

Ann Summers sex shop opens in Princes Street during Church of Scotland General Assembly

Sir Mark Thatcher arrested, accused of being involved in a plot to overthrow African dictator

Gilmerton Cove, once used as a drinking den, is opened to the public

A bearded man in a dress gatecrashes Prince William's birthday party at Windsor Castle –
Robin Cook still asking questions about Iraq.

Protests over Bank of Scotland plans to close the head office on the Mound.

Months after the overthrow of Saddam, millions of Iraqis still have no access to clean water or electricity

A delegation from Edinburgh including Lord Provost Eric Milligan go to Rome to see Cardinal Keith O'Brien's inauguration
– Hearts reach the next round of the UEFA Cup.

Sex & the City author Candace Bushnell appears at the Edinburgh Book Festival

Michael Howard, whose parents were from Transylvania, is still tainted by his connections to Margaret Thatcher.

As British Telecom outsource their call centres to India, will others follow?

Edinburgh and Glasgow are urged to work together to attract tourists

Edinburgh's Lord Provost Eric Milligan visits Paris to celebrate the Auld Alliance.

Edinburgh Dungeon opens Glencoe exhibition – Margo McDonald is expelled from SNP.

Edinburgh City Council bans Happy Hours. Hearts lose heavily to Hibs.

Nestlé's condensed milk, a crucial ingredient of tablet, ends production in the UK.

Contaminated ships are sent from USA to Britain to be broken up despite protests from environmentalists.

Hoover close Scottish plant and move production to China.

George Bush stays with the Queen at Buckingham Palace.

'Restoration' a programme about restoring old buildings starts on TV.

The Scottish Executive's attempt to improve the nation's diet meets with a poor response.

Jack McConnell falls on icy steps outside Bute House.

Dungavel Detention Centre is heavily criticised.

2004

Virgin Trains announce plans to introduce Pendolino tilting trains on the main Glasgow-London route.

Treasures of the Romanovs exhibition opens at the National Museum of Scotland.

Jack McConnell decides to play golf rather than meet D-Day veterans.

Plans to extend Edinburgh's parking zone are opposed by Marchmont residents.

Shadow Chancellor Oliver Letwin proposes a £35billion cut in public spending.

It is suggested that Hearts might play Celtic in Australia.

Plans are unveiled for a continental-style waterfront development at Granton.

SNP leadership contest held amid poor election results – Wet Wet Wet make a comeback.

Local residents complain about rubbish floating on the Water of Leith.

A delegation of Scottish politicians including Donald Gorrie, David McLetchie and John Swinney attend Tartan Day parade in New York.

Residents of Edinburgh's New Town resist the introduction of wheelie bins.

Staff complain about heat in the new Edinburgh Royal Infirmary.

The US 'liberation' of Fallujah results in massive destruction of the city.

Alex Neil stands down as a candidate in SNP leadership election in the week that Marlon Brando dies.

The end of Lord Fraser's enquiry into Holyrood building – Mel Gibson's 'Passion of Christ' comes out on DVD.

Hibs announce that Elton John is to play a concert at Easter Road.

Concerts at the Castle Esplanade featuring Meat Loaf and Bob Dylan are cancelled.

Council Leader Donald Anderson keeps transport chief Councillor Andrew Burns in his post despite the costly defeat in Edinburgh's road tolls referendum.

Rudi Giuliani says that Bush was like Churchill.

Royal Navy recognises Satanism as a religion.

Tory leader David McLetchie is heavily involved in campaign against road tolls.

Rev Ian Paisley still says No to power-sharing with Sinn Fein.

Justice Minister Cathy Jamieson urges the Co-op in Auchinleck to stop selling Buckfast.
Another branch plays classical music to drive away loitering youths.

Lothian & Borders police officers are urged to lose weight.

Ronald Reagan dies.

Jenners is sold to House of Fraser.

Jack McConnell suggests that BBC Children's TV should move to Glasgow.

With trams planned for Edinburgh, what other transport schemes could be built?

Director of the National Gallery Sir Tim Clifford wants two ice-cream vans removed from outside the building – the Playfair project linking the two galleries on the Mound by underground tunnel is under construction.

Jim Wallace stands down as Scottish Lib-Dem leader.

Transport Minister Alistair Darling opens a Guided Busway.
The first solar-powered bus shelter is installed.

Plans are announced to reintroduce beavers into Scotland.

Edinburgh's 2005 Hogmanay celebrations will have a Catalan theme.
The architect of the new Scottish Parliament building was from Barcelona.

Oor Wullie is voted Scotland's top icon – Jack McConnell falls out with Sir Sean Connery but meets him in New York.

Riots in Belfast after 12th July parades.

'Feed the World' re-released to celebrate 20th anniversary of Band Aid.

Michael Howard still sticks to right wing policies.

Greece surprisingly win the European Football Championship.

David Blunkett gets tough on asylum seekers

2005

Knitting classes were held in a pub in Leith.

Scottish Tory Leader David McLetchie resigned following revelations that he had used his parliamentary taxi account for personal trips.

Obesity reaches new levels in USA.

Born-again Christian George W Bush finds his popularity slipping.

The matronly Annabel Goldie is elected leader of the Scottish Tories with Murdo Fraser as her deputy.

Kenny Richey, the Scot on Death Row in America, suffers a further setback
when the Supreme Court overturns a previous decision to release him.

Turner Prize is won by an artist who dismantled a shed and sailed it down the River Rhine.

Scottish children are now the fattest in the world.

During the General Election, Michael Howard made comments regarded as offensive to the travelling community.

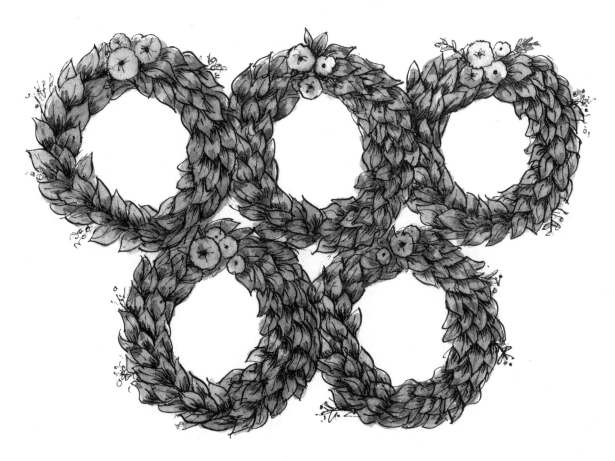

On July 6th London is awarded the Olympics for 2012.
The following day four bombs explode killing 52 people.

Michael Howard is accused of gutter politics during the election campaign.
Tory slogan is 'Are you thinking what we're thinking.'

Workers in the financial sector are allowed to dress casually to avoid detection by anarchists during G8 demonstrations.

The unsuccessful attempt to introduce road tolls costs taxpayers £9million.

New series of 'I'm a Celebrity, Get Me Out of Here' starts on TV –
Scottish Executive vows to tackle sectarianism.

Police try to clear beggars from the Royal Mile.

Irvine Welsh claims he was inspired by Jane Austen.

The Old Firm are urged to end sectarian singing.

Cherie Blair's purchase of two flats in Bristol is handled by a convicted conman.

Tony Blair refuses to break his Caribbean holiday to attend Robin Cook's funeral.

Gruesome pictures are published of British troops abusing Iraqi prisoners.

Gail Sheridan has a baby.

Midge Ure urges Edinburgh residents to welcome G8 protesters into their homes.

Cambridge University bans students from wearing kilts at graduation ceremonies.

Both Hearts and Hibs lose Scottish Cup semifinals –
Cardinal O'Brien is in Rome for the election of a new Pope.

Jack McConnell plays a minor role during the G8 summit at Gleneagles.

Hibs qualify for European football while Hearts miss out.

Roll Harris paints the Queen's portrait.
England beat Australia to win The Ashes.

Metropolitan police shoot an innocent Brazilian at Stockwell Underground station.

2006

The smoking ban comes into effect in Scotland's pubs.

No police officers will be charged with the death of innocent Brazilian, Jean Charles De Menezes, shot at Stockwell Tube station in 2005.

US billionaire Donald Trump wants to build a golf course in Scotland despite protests from environmentalists.

George Bush said America is addicted to oil.

UEFA initially refused to punish Rangers fans for sectarian singing on the grounds that it had been tolerated for years in Scotland.

Tony Blair said God would judge him over the invasion of Iraq.

The Labour Party spent £7,700 on Cherie Blair's hair during the 2005 election campaign.

Hearts win the Scottish Cup. Illusionist David Blaine spent several days under water in a tank.

US Marines massacre civilians at Haditha and attempt to cover it up.

Irvine Welsh writes a play about the Munchkins from the Wizard of Oz.

Irvine Welsh admits he had benefited from Thatcherism and that the admired David Cameron.

Jack McConnell says he would be supporting Trinidad & Tobago during the World Cup.

Scots are criticised in the English press for not supporting England in the World Cup.

Sir Sean Connery pulls out of an interview with George Reid after the Presiding Officer says he would ask him tough questions on his attitude to women.

The Scottish Executive bans the sale of swords, including Samurai swords.

Two Asian men are forced to leave a plane after their passengers fear they might be suicide bombers. Tony Blair is on holiday in Barbados.

It is alleged that the CIA are flying prisoners to secret jails via Prestwick airport.

Despite receiving millions in government grants, US computer firm Lexmark closes its inkjet printer factory in Rosyth with the loss of 700 jobs.

Hearts oppose plans to expand a legal cocaine manufacturing plant next to their ground.

Jack McConnell launches Scotland's bid for the 2014 Commonwealth Games at a swimming pool in Glasgow.
Celtic lose 2-1 to Clyde in the Scottish Cup.

A report reveals that Leith and surrounding areas have some of the lowest life expectancies in Edinburgh. Hibs lose 4-1 to Hearts.

Glasgow bids for a super casino – Obesity reaches record levels in Scotland.

Visit Frank Boyle's website
www.boylecartoon.co.uk
email: info@boylecartoon.co.uk